3

WILD HORSES

Wild Horse Magic for Kids

To Dr. Jay F. Kirkpatrick and others like him, who have given so much of themselves to make sure that wild horses will always have places to roam wild and free.

– Mark Henckel

For a free color catalog describing Gareth Stevens' list of high-quality books, call 1-800-542-2595 (USA) or 1-800-461-9120 (Canada). Gareth Stevens' Fax: 414-225-0377.

Library of Congress Cataloging-in-Publication Data

Henckel, Mark.
    Wild horses: wild horse magic for kids / by Mark Henckel ; photography by Michael H. Francis ; illustrated by John F. McGee.
        p. cm. — (Animal magic for kids)
    Based on: Wild horses for kids. 1995.
    Includes index.
    Summary: Presents information about wild horses through the conversation of ten-year-old April, who is vacationing in the West, and the cowboy she meets.
    ISBN-0-8368-1378-2
    1. Wild horses—North America—Juvenile literature. [1. Wild horses. 2. Horses.] I. Francis, Michael H. (Michael Harlowe), 1953- ill. II. McGee, John F., ill. III. Henckel, Mark. Wild horses for kids. IV. Title. V. Series.
SF360.3.N7H46.   1995
599.7'25—dc20   95-16312

This edition first published in 1995 by
Gareth Stevens Publishing
1555 North RiverCenter Drive, Suite 201
Milwaukee, Wisconsin 53212 USA

Based on the book, *Wild Horses for Kids*, text © 1995 by Mark Henckel, photographs © 1995 by Michael H. Francis, with illustrations by John F. McGee. First published in the United States in 1995 by NorthWord Press, Inc., Minocqua, Wisconsin. End matter © 1995 by Gareth Stevens, Inc.

Printed in the United States of America

1 2 3 4 5 6 7 8 9 99 98 97 96 95

by Mark Henckel

WILD HORSES

Wild Horse Magic for Kids

Gareth Stevens Publishing
MILWAUKEE

"Are you a real cowboy?"

The small voice took Matt by surprise. He stopped walking. He tipped his cowboy hat back on his head. He turned and looked down the sidewalk at a young girl who was sitting in a wheelchair.

"What did you say?" he asked.

"Are you a real cowboy?" the girl asked again. "You look like a real cowboy. You've got the hat, the boots, and the blue jeans. So, are you a real cowboy?"

"I guess I am a cowboy, sort of," Matt said, with a laugh. "My dad owns a ranch. I herd some cows for him when I'm not in school or playing baseball. And I'm fifteen, so I guess I'm still a boy. Yeah, that makes me a cowboy. My name is Matt. What's yours?"

"My name is April, and I'm ten," she said. "But I don't have much time. I'm here on vacation with my folks. I have to find a cowboy fast. I need one to take me to see some real wild horses."

"Well, nice to meet you April," Matt said, tipping his hat and bending to shake her hand. "Now, what's this about wild horses?"

April told him that she *loved* wild horses. That's why she talked her parents into driving out West on vacation. She had looked and looked out the car window all the way to this small western town and she still hadn't seen any. Now her parents were busy shopping for souvenirs and she was out here on the sidewalk hoping to meet a cowboy so he could find her some wild horses.

"I love wild horses! I started reading about them in the library at school," April said. "Then I got all the books I could at the library downtown.

"The more I read about wild horses, the more I liked them," she said, "and the more I dreamed about coming out West to see them."

Matt sat down next to her on the curb.

"Well," he said. "You know wild horses aren't just everywhere, even out here in the West. We do have some near here. And I know a little bit about wild horses. But I only know what I've seen when I was lucky enough to spot them. They're not easy to see. They live in the rugged, dry hills outside of town. They're some tough critters."

April said she knew that wild horses were tough. She knew they got their start in North America almost 500 years ago. The first horses came with Christopher Columbus in 1493 when he sailed to the New World on one of his trips here from Spain.

The 25 horses he brought with him ended up on an island in the Caribbean. Another Spanish explorer, Hernando Cortez, brought 17 horses with him to Mexico in 1519. Other horses came with other explorers and settlers.

Some of those first horses in America escaped from their owners. Others were let go on purpose. In both cases, the horses became wild horses. And they liked what they found—plenty of grass, plenty of places to run and plenty of room to breed.

By the 1700s, there were millions of wild horses in North America, especially on the big grassy plains of central North America and the mountains and deserts of the West. There were wild horses as far west as California and Oregon, as far north as British Columbia and Alberta in Canada, and as far south as Mexico.

"Only a few explorers saw the wild horse bands of the West back then," April said. "But it didn't take long for Native Americans to catch horses and tame them.

14

"Indian tribes like the Sioux, Crow, Cheyenne, Nez Perce, Shoshone and Comanche used horses a lot," she said. "They didn't need saddles or bridles to ride them, either. All they needed was a blanket on the horse's back and a horsehair rope around the horse's jaw."

April told Matt that Indians rode horses when they hunted buffalo, and when they rode into battle. They used horses to carry things and drag their teepees and other belongings when they moved to new camps.

The number of horses that an Indian had also told how rich he was. Having a lot of good, fast horses meant that they could win races, bring meat home and protect themselves.

"The books said things started to change for the wild horses when settlers came West," April said. "They needed the land where the wild horses lived to make their farms and to raise cattle."

Wild horses were pushed to lands not good enough for farming or ranching.

"That's for sure," Matt agreed. "My grandfather told me that there used to be a lot more wild horses around here than there are now. He called them nothing but trouble because they'd get in his fields and break down his fences."

"So they caught wild horses and sold them, to make money and to just get rid of them," Matt said. "If they could tame the horses, they used some of them for riding and some of them for farming. They sold some of them for rodeos. During World War I, they even sold some to the Army."

Matt said that to find wild horses now, you'd have to go into the dry hills where only a few animals live, like mule deer and pronghorn antelope.

"Yes," April said. "There used to be millions of wild horses. I've read there are only about 50,000 left."

"Most of them are out here in the West in parts of Nevada, California, Oregon, Utah, Colorado, North Dakota, Wyoming and Montana," she said. "But did you know there are some wild horses on islands in the Atlantic Ocean, too? There's one island

called Assateague, off the Maryland
and Virginia coast, where there
have been wild horses for 360 years.
There are also some on the
Shackleford Banks, off North
Carolina, and on Cumberland
Island, off the Georgia coast, too.
Bet you didn't know that."

23

"Did you know they eat a lot of different plants, depending on where they live," she added. "They eat a lot of different kinds of grasses and even shrubs and trees, if they have to. They can even eat poison ivy.

"And, depending on where you find them, they can come in all different colors. You can find brown horses, buckskin, gray, black, pinto. Some horses in some places even have special marks like striping on their legs."

April sure was smart, especially for a ten-year-old, Matt thought. She knew a lot about wild horses.

"You said you saw some wild horses here. Tell me about them," April said.

"They're really pretty amazing," Matt said. "You have to be real sneaky to see them up close. I found that out the hard way.

"Sometimes, when I was done with my chores and homework, and wasn't playing baseball, I'd go riding in the dry hills. I'd go looking for those horses," he said. "It took me a while to figure them out."

Matt told April that the first times he went riding to look for wild horses, he only saw them far in the distance. Whenever he tried to get close to them, they'd always see him first. They would run away and hide by the time he got there.

"They really have good eyesight," Matt said. "They can see you coming from a long way off."

Matt started to take binoculars along on his rides. That way, he could spot them from far away. Then, he'd plan a way to sneak closer and find a place where he could hide and watch them.

Sometimes, he'd spend hours watching those horses from his hiding spots. He told April that the horses were found in groups called harem bands. Most of the harem bands had five to seven horses in them. Some had as many as twenty traveling together.

The harem bands have an older male horse, a mature stallion. They also have older females, the mature mares. Then there are the young one- and two-year-olds.

During the breeding season—sometime between March and July—the stallion rules the group. During the rest of the year, one of the older mares leads the band. She's called the lead mare.

Other horse groups, called bachelor bands, are made up only of young stallions that aren't old enough yet to have any mares of their own.

"You can see a lot of different things when you really spend some time watching wild horses," Matt said. "The stallion, for example, will fight off the younger males. By the time they get old, some of those stallions have a lot of scars on them from being bitten or cut by other horses' hooves.

"When they fight, the stallions will scream, bite and kick until one of them just gives up and runs away," he said.

Matt told her that most of the foals, the baby horses, are born in the months of April and May. When they're born, the foals' bodies look really small and their legs look really long and weak.

"But by the time they're just an hour or two old, they're up on their feet. They come to their mothers looking for milk. It almost seems like they're born hungry," he said.

"It doesn't take long for them to learn how to walk and then to run. That's the best part, watching the young horses run," Matt said. "They kick, jump, play and run in circles. They play like they're fighting, then they start running again.

"That happens during the summer. It's the happiest time of the year. The saddest time is during the winter," he said.

That surprised April. "Winter is sad? Why is it sad?" she asked.

"You never think about it much, but winter is the time of year when wild horses are most likely to die," Matt said. "Wild horses are so tough that they can live through a lot of things. They can live in the summer even when it's hotter than 100 degrees. When it doesn't rain and it's really dry, people call that a drought. Wild horses can live through that. They just paw down into the mud in old water holes and still find water. But winter out here is really dangerous.

"In some winters, I've seen snow that piled so deep it was up to their bellies," Matt said. "Sometimes, it gets so cold that the temperature can be 30 or 40 degrees below zero. When the snow covers their food and the temperature gets real cold, some horses die. It's usually the young, the old, the sick, and the weak horses that are in the most danger.

42

"But the good news is that wild horses have been through it before. They've survived the heat, the drought, the snow and the cold in the West for hundreds of years. Even though some of them will die, others will live to see spring and summer come again."

Matt added that it was all part of nature. But even if they did have to die, he told April that the important thing was that wild horses were still living, too. They were wild and free in the wide open spaces of the West and in places like Assateague Island in the East. Just like 500 years ago, there were still places for wild horses to call home and places for people to go see them. That's what was really important.

"That's really true," April said. "You know, I'm in a wheelchair. But somehow, it makes me feel better when I think about those horses. I can close my eyes and use my imagination and see them running in the hills, racing as fast as their legs will carry them.

"I guess that's why it's my dream to see them and to ride a horse someday soon," she said.

GLOSSARY

Bachelor band: A group of wild horses made up of young stallions without mares (page 33).

Breed (v): To produce offspring; to reproduce (page 13).

Buckskin: A horse that is light yellow-brown in color, usually with a dark mane and tail (page 24).

Drought: A period of little or no rain (page 42).

Foal: A young horse or related animal (page 39).

Harem band: A group of wild horses that includes a mature stallion and a number of mares of different ages (page 30).

Hooves: Feet that are covered with a tough, protective covering of horn (page 35).

Mare: A female horse or related animal, such as a zebra (page 32).

Mature: Fully grown or developed (page 32).

Pinto: A spotted horse or pony (page 24).

Plains: A large, flat, grassy area of land without trees (page 14).

Rugged: Difficult or rough (page 9).

Settlers: In this book, people who came to the New World from European countries (page 13).

Shrub: A woody plant smaller than a tree (page 24).

Stallion: A mature male horse (page 32).

ADULT-CHILD INTERACTION QUESTIONS

These are questions designed to encourage young readers to participate in further study and discussion of wild horses.

1. Do wild horses live in other parts of the world other than North America? Where can they be found, and what are they called?

2. How did the Spaniards transport horses to the New World?

3. How much vegetation does a wild horse eat each day?

4. Are there programs to help protect wild horses and conserve their habitat?

5. What were the ancestors of today's wild horses like?

6. How do wild horses differ from domesticated horses, such as thoroughbreds or quarterhorses?

7. How did the American Indians capture wild horses that they later domesticated?

8. If you were a wild horse, how would you feel if you encountered a group of humans?

9. Use a map to find the islands off the east coast of the United States where wild horses can be found.

MORE BOOKS TO READ

A Closer Look at Horses by Neil Thompson (Franklin Watts)
Horses by Elsa Posell (Childrens Press)
Horses and Foals by Fern Brown (Franklin Watts)
The Last Wild Horse by Morris Weeks (Houghton Mifflin)
Misty of Chincoteague by Marguerite Henry (Macmillan)
The Wild Horses by Carl Green and William Sanford (Crestwood House)
Wild Horses by Carol Ann Moorhead (Roberts Rinehart)
Zoobooks: Wild Horses by John Bonnett Wexo (Wildlife Education Ltd.)

VIDEOS

Horse (Barr Films)
Horse (Media Guild)
Horses! (Encyclopedia Britannica Educational)